Frogs!

Elizabeth Carney

SCHOLASTIC INC.
New York Toronto London Auckland
Sydney Mexico City New Delhi Hong Kong

ISBN 978-0-545-25179-2

48 47 46 45 44 43   17/0

Printed in the U.S.A.   40

First Scholastic printing, April 2010

Table of Contents

Splash!

Pacific Chorus Frog

Q What happened to the frog's car when it broke down?

A It got toad.

Splish, splash.

What is that sound?

What is hopping and
jumping around?

What loves to swim?

What loves to eat bugs?

It's a frog!

Can you hop like a frog?

Frogs live all over the world, except Antarctica. Frogs usually live in wet places. They like rivers, lakes, and ponds.

Marsh Frog

Andean Marsupial Frog

Antarctica is the continent at the South Pole.

Ribbit!

Habitat: The natural place where a plant or animal lives

Red-Eyed Tree Frog

Bullfrog

But some frogs live in trees. Some even live in the desert. Frogs can be found all over the world. Wherever they live, that's their habitat.

Croak!

Look at this frog croaking! Some frogs' throats puff up when they make sounds. Each type of frog makes its own sound.

Lake Frog

Ribbit!

Croak: The deep, hoarse noise that a frog makes

Coqui Frog

The coqui frog is named after the sound it makes. It sounds like "CO-KEE!" This frog is the size of a quarter. Even small frogs can make loud noises.

Frogs make different sounds
for different reasons. Sometimes
it's to warn other frogs of
danger. Sometimes it's to call
to frogs nearby.

Dancing Frog

This frog lives around
noisy waterfalls. Other
frogs would not be able
to hear its calls. So it
dances instead! It sticks
out one leg, and then the
other. Can you dance
like this frog?

Frog Food

What is a frog's favorite food? Usually it's insects. Frogs eat dragonflies and crickets and other bugs.

Green Frog

Q Why are frogs so happy?

A They eat what bugs them!

Amazon Horned Frog

Some frogs eat bigger animals like worms and mice. The American bullfrog even eats other frogs!

American Bullfrog

What's that pink flash? It's how a frog catches bugs. It shoots out its long, sticky tongue at a passing bug. The frog pulls the bug into its mouth.

If your tongue were as long as a frog's, it would reach to your belly button!

Green Tree Frog

Every Size and Color

Frogs can be many different sizes.

Microfrog

The smallest frog is as
big as a fingernail.
The largest is as big as a rabbit.

Goliath Frog

Frogs can be different colors, too.

Tiger Striped Leaf Frog

Some are green or brown.

Amazonian Poison Dart Frog

Others have stripes or spots.

Red Poison Dart Frog

Frogs can be red, yellow, or orange.

Blue Poison Dart Frog

They can even be bright blue!

Watch Out!

These colorful frogs may look pretty. But watch out! These frogs have poison in their skin. Their bright color warns enemies not to eat them.

Poison Dart Frog

Ribbit!

Poison:
Something that can kill or hurt living things

Poison Dart Frog

Yellow Banded Poison Dart Frog

This little frog is only an inch long. Its name is Terribilis, which means "the terrible one." How did it get this name? By being the most deadly frog of all! One Terribilis has enough poison to kill 20,000 mice.

Terribilis

Red-Eyed Tree Frog Eggs

Frog Babies

All frogs, even the Terribilis, have mothers. Mother frogs lay eggs. When the eggs are ready, out pop the tadpoles!

Tadpoles are baby frogs. But they don't look like frogs yet. Tadpoles have tails. They live only in water.

Pacific Tree Frog Tadpole

Tadpoles grow up to be frogs.

1 At first they breathe underwater with gills.

gills

Tadpoles

Red-Eyed Tree Frog Tadpoles

Ribbit!

Gills: The body parts on the sides of a fish or tadpole through which it breathes

2 They grow lungs for breathing air.

3 They grow legs for hopping and swimming.

Monkey Frog Tadpole

4 In three months, they lose their tails.

Bullfrog

It's time to hop out of the water!

Toads Are Frogs, Too!

What's the difference between toads and frogs?

FROG

Some frogs are poisonous.

Moist and smooth

Teeth in upper jaw

Long, powerful jumping legs; most frogs have webbed hind feet.

Eggs laid in clusters, or groups

Toads are a type of frog. Frogs spend most of their lives around water. Toads spend more time on dry land. Their bodies are built for where they live.

TOAD

Eyes do not bulge out from the body; a poison gland is located behind each eye.

Dry and bumpy

No teeth

Eggs laid in long chains (but a few toads give birth to live young)

Shorter legs (for walking)

THE SCREAMER

LOUD-MOUTHED FROG LEAVES ENEMIES STUNNED!

AAAAAA-II-EEEE!!!

MR. INVISIBLE

HE'S A MASTER OF DISGUISE!

Now you see him. Now you don't!

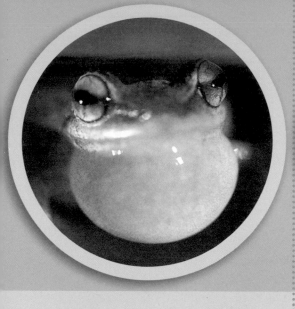

gills

CROAK
The deep, hoarse noise that a frog makes

GILLS
The body parts on the sides of a fish or tadpole through which it breathes

HABITAT
The natural place where a plant or animal lives

POISON
Something that can kill or hurt living things